URI GELLER

Learn to Dowse

USE THE WORLD'S MOST POWERFUL SEARCH ENGINE: YOUR INTUITION

This edition first published in the UK and USA in 2020 by
Watkins, an imprint of Watkins Media Limited
Unit 11, Shepperton House
89-93 Shepperton Road
London
N1 3DF
enquiries@watkinspublishing.com

Design and typography copyright © Watkins Media Limited 2020

Text copyright © Uri Geller 2006, 2020

1 2 3 4 5 6 7 8 9 10

Designed and Typeset by Watkins

Printed and bound in the United Kingdom

A CIP record for this book is available from the British Library

ISBN: 978-1-78678-382-0

www.watkinspublishing.com

URI GELLER

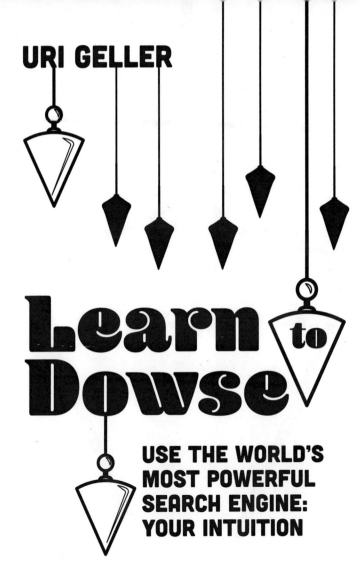

Learn to Dowse

USE THE WORLD'S MOST POWERFUL SEARCH ENGINE: YOUR INTUITION

WATKINS
Sharing Wisdom Since 1893

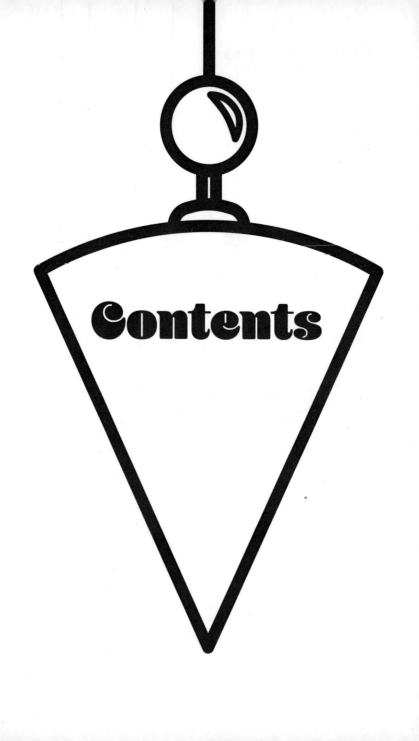

Contents

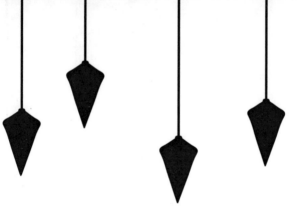

Introduction

WHAT IS DOWSING?

The three main dowsing tools are the Y-shaped twig, metal dowsing rods and the crystal pendulum. But you can also dowse with just your hands.

Dowsing isn't just something I do. It's everything I do. Everyone can dowse. Like language, it's an innate ability that reveals itself as we learn. Human beings were dowsing long before we could write: there are cave paintings 6,500 years old, in the Tassili n'Ajjer mountains of the eastern Sahara, that are believed to depict a dowser using a bent stick (*see* opposite). That's long before Stonehenge, long before Troy, earlier even than Noah and the Ark.

Dowsing is a method of searching by intuition. Instead of relying on the five senses, a dowser uses the power of the mind. It's widely regarded as a psychic method of looking for water, but that's just one use of dowsing – as you learn to harness your innate talent, you'll discover you can dowse to find lost objects, buried relics, hidden minerals and natural energy sources. Most important of all, you can use dowsing to unlock the submerged

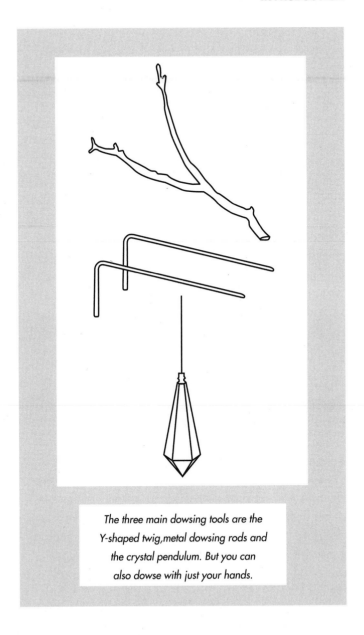

*The three main dowsing tools are the
Y-shaped twig, metal dowsing rods and
the crystal pendulum. But you can
also dowse with just your hands.*

thoughts, knowledge and intuitions in your own mind, and you will learn how to evaluate vital choices in business, love and family life. The book you are holding will teach you this timeless skill.

Conscious thought is just a tiny fraction of what our brains do. Our incredible senses process far more information than ever breaks the surface of our minds, but our bodies do react to it. By dowsing, we can read those reactions.

The Y-shaped twig is just one tool that responds to subconscious thought and psychic awareness. A pair of L-shaped rods, a crystal suspended by a thread and the tingling sensation in our hands can all be invaluable indicators. I'll explain how to perfect the techniques of using each of these.

I'll also explore the science behind dowsing, a combination of biology, psychology and physics. There's nothing supernatural about dowsing: it's a physical phenomenon, a human ability employed by the British and US armies as well as every major oil corporation and water provider.

Look out for my mini-classes – unique exercises to enhance your DQ, or Dowsing Quotient. And turn to the true stories for inspirational tales of great dowsing achievements. I believe we learn best and remember most when we're having fun. This book is packed with dowsing games, and all the exercises are designed to be entertaining – in fact, every page is full of fun.

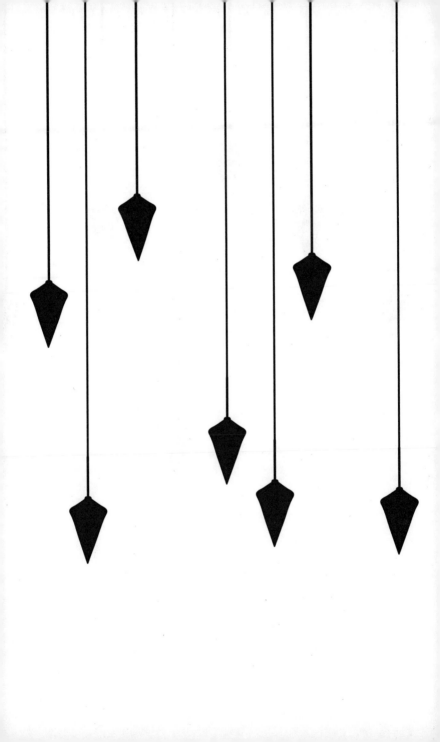

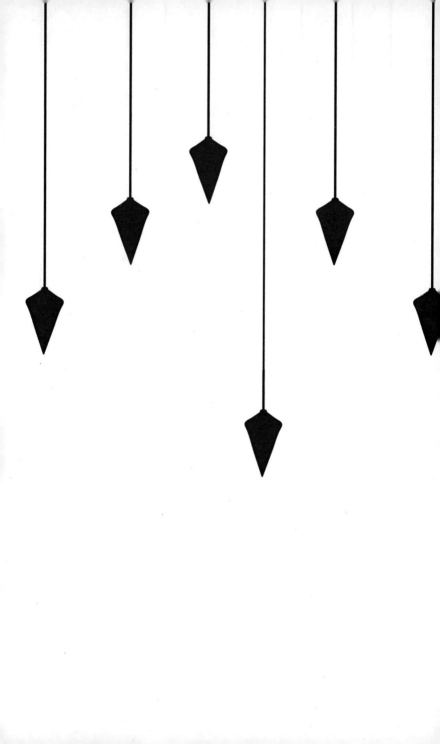

BASIC PRINCIPLES

HOW TO DOWSE WITH A CRYSTAL PENDULUM

A crystal pendulum is a superb tool to unlock the subconscious. Anyone can learn to use it instantly, but the depth of wisdom it can reveal will sustain you throughout your life.

A pendulum is simply a weight, or "bobber", suspended by a chain or thread about 6–9in (15–22cm) long, which is held between your thumb and forefinger. My pendulum is a piece of Brazilian crystal, suspended from a gold pocket-watch chain more than a century old, given to me by the silent-screen diva Gloria Swanson. We met in New York in the mid1970s – she heard about this young Israeli who was into health food and the paranormal, two of her passions, and she invited me to her apartment. We became good friends, and she made me a gift of the chain, which had belonged to her great-grandfather.

A rock crystal is the perfect tool for pendulum dowsing. It's a simple device, capable of the most complex subtlety. Millions of years old, it acts like a natural radio receiver to focus the energy of your mind.

Hold it so the bobber hangs in front of your solar plexus, below your ribcage. When your mind is empty, the bobber hangs motionless; but if you frame a question in your mind, the pendulum will start to swing.

To understand the messages your pendulum sends, you must learn to speak its language. Ask a clear, simple question – "Is today Friday?" "Is my name Uri?" – and watch how the pendulum responds. My bobber swings in a wide circle to answer "Yes", and switches to a back-and-forth arc when the answer is "No".

Don't worry if nothing happens at first. Keep practising: the moment your pendulum first moves is unforgettable, a taste of magic. Always ask questions that can be answered "Yes" or "No". Practise in peaceful solitude at first – you'll soon find you have the confidence to consult your pendulum when others are around, even when the room is noisy.

I first used a pendulum after my mentor, Dr Andrija Puharich, told me how the Mayan Indians of Mexico had communicated with their gods using this tool. Andrija believed the pendulum's messages came from a higher intelligence, perhaps an extraterrestrial energy. But today I believe the force that moves the pendulum comes from within our own bodies. By seeking answers from the pendulum, we are freeing knowledge in our own subconscious, accessing layers of the mind that cannot be reached by thought alone.

True stories

I saw a dramatic demonstration of pendulum power in Venice while shooting my Haunted Cities show. I was exploring a mansion, Palazzo Ca'Dario, reputed to be cursed. With my pendulum swinging from my left hand, I asked to see evidence that a malign force was resident in the building.

"Will I find proof in this room?" I asked. The pendulum swung in a circle: yes. "Is it by this bookcase?" Back and forth: no. "By the mantelpiece?" Round and round: yes. A scrap of paper poking between two bricks in the mantel caught my eye, and I pulled out a faded, frayed photograph. The back stated "Egypt, 1941". The picture showed a desiccated, mummified body.

That was evidence enough. I felt an overpowering malevolence all around me. I ordered the camera crew to follow me and we ran from the building. They wanted to stay, but I knew that if we did we would be putting our psychic safety, and perhaps even our sanity, in peril.

HOW TO DOWSE WITH RODS

Watch a beetle or a snail as it climbs a twig. Its antennae are constantly probing, sensing the vibrations and currents of energy all around. Now take some L-shaped copper rods and hold them lightly in your outstretched fists.

These are your antennae.

Hold those rods by the short stem, just tightly enough to stop them from spinning around when you move your hands. Keep your elbows bent, slightly away from your sides, and your hands at chest height.

Our instincts are most keenly attuned to fresh, running water so, for your first experiment, take your rods somewhere outside where you can dowse undisturbed.

Your garden, a peaceful park, a safe countryside beauty spot, even the beach: these are all great places to start.

Form an image in your mind of what you're dowsing for. This is sometimes called visualization, but really it's nothing more psychic than imagination. Picture a current of running water under the ground. It could be a subterranean stream or the mains water supply.

Keeping that image in your mind and holding the rods gently, walk around slowly. To intensify your focus, you could ask aloud: "Is there water here?"

When you walk over a water course, the rods will unmistakably twitch and cross, or else leap apart. That's a thrilling moment, because you will know that you did not consciously provoke the reaction. The effect is instantaneous: your confidence in your ability to dowse, what we call your Dowsing Quotient, or DQ for short, will soar.

However many times you dowse, you'll never forget your first success. It's life-changing.

Uri's mini-class

You can turn yourself into a human compass with your angle rods. Command them to point north and they will swing toward the magnetic pole. Oddly, my left hand finds north without fail, but my right hand gets it wrong by 180 degrees and points south. Does this give us a clue to how migrating birds find their way?

9

HOW TO DOWSE WITH A FORKED STICK

Dowsing with a forked stick is the oldest method of divining. It's also the one I don't use. My hands are sensitive and I find a twig just gets in the way – a bit like wearing spectacles if you have perfect vision. A lens that puts the world into focus for one person might render everything impossibly blurred for another. Perhaps you're like me – or perhaps a wand will turn you into a Hogwarts graduate. There's only one way to find out and that's to experiment. Everything about dowsing is practical.

It's important to respect your dowsing rod. This is not a broken branch, it is an extension of your psyche. Before you take your pruning shears to a tree, first ask the tree's permission by saying a prayer of thanks for the natural wonders we so often ignore. If you suddenly feel uncomfortable about lopping a branch off this particular tree, move on – the tree is denying its permission! But if you feel a thrill of admiration for this living marvel that has grown from a seed with invisible slowness, you have found a tree in harmony with your own spirit and most probably you'll dowse well with it.

Choose a supple, forked branch, with prongs about 18in (46cm) long and a pointer of 4in (10cm). If possible, choose the branch by moonlight and come back in the morning to cut it. This ritual emphasizes your commitment to dowsing as a serious, spiritual activity. Trim the buds and twigs, and hold the two forked ends in your hands, palms upward. Rest your thumbs along the wood, and

bend the forks out slightly. With your elbows at your sides, point the tip of the stick a little up from level.

Now start dowsing! With an image of running water in your mind, explore your garden, the park, a field or anywhere that seems peaceful and promising. When your rod reacts, you'll know: many dowsers say the stick suddenly gains a life of its own, twisting so vigorously in your hands that it can strip its own bark. The most common response is the "dip", where the pointer dives to indicate the spot where underground water runs. Some dowsers report their tip jerks upward, and others find they work best with the rod clasped near the fork, or with their palms facing down rather than up. One of the most celebrated dowsers, the Victorian William Stokes, held his rod down vertically.

If you love tools and gadgets, you might appreciate a human-made dowsing rod called an aurameter. Developed in the 1940s by Verne L Cameron, it comprises a handle with a spring at one end. A wire wand protrudes from the spring, with a weighted pointer on the tip. It looks a little like something you'd use to light a gas stove, but enthusiasts say it's uniquely versatile: the bobber searches from side to side like a bloodhound on a trail, it oscillates like a pendulum and it dives like a dowsing rod.

True stories

In 2017 science blogger Sally Le Page asked all 12 of the UK's water companies if their engineers dowsed for underground pipes and water sources. Her curiosity was piqued after her parents reported seeing a technician from their local water company using "bent tent pegs" to locate the mains water pipes near their home. To her surprise, 10 out of 12 water companies confirmed that their engineers sometimes used dowsing rods, with Severn Trent adding that while they also use drones and satellites, "We've found that some of the older methods are just as effective".

MIND-POWER TECHNIQUES

Dowsing with a pendulum is one of the most relaxing and calming of all mind-power techniques. Telepathy might leave me feeling confused, spoon-bending can be exhausting, but a few minutes with my eyes and my spirit focused on the moving crystal are as good as deep meditation. It's important to use your dowsing ability frequently if your powers are to develop, so instead of turning to the crystal or the rods only when you need to find an answer, pick them up for fun and relaxation.

When you're feeling tired or low, ask your crystal to give its positive response. I hold mine and simply say, "Show me 'Yes'", and it starts to trace an anticlockwise path. After a minute or two, it's whirling like a fairground ride, though my hand seems to be still as rock. My mind floats to a calm, alert state where my hearing is enhanced and my thoughts are uncluttered. If my stomach was knotted with tension or my heartbeat was too quick, all that negativity disperses. It's like a hot, perfumed bath for the soul.

Your crystal will enjoy a bath too. Wherever you keep it, in a box, on a shelf or in your pocket, it will sometimes be exposed to negative energy, even if it's just picking up and absorbing your emotions as you watch the evening news on television. You can rinse this negative residue away by holding the stone under warm running water. Visualize fierce energy blazing like fiery phosphorous all around your hands and the crystal, and say a simple prayer: "I release all negative energy to the void, where it will turn to vapour and cause no harm."

Uri's mini-class

To clear your mind before dowsing, try this thought experiment. Imagine you are walking across the plush carpet of an elegant hotel lobby. Outside, the chaotic city is swarming, but here you are in an oasis of calm and order. You are walking to the elevator, where an attendant in spotless livery holds the door. That attendant is me!

I gaze straight into your eyes and I say, "This elevator will carry your mind to a high pinnacle of focus and clarity. We will be riding up a towering spire, soaring above the

clouds, to where the sky is always clear and the air is like a draught of icy, fresh water. Will you step inside?"

You walk into the lift and, as I press the button, you see an orange counter that lights up above the door. "At each floor, you will become twice as focused as you were before," you hear me say softly and with complete authority. You trust my voice.

"Going up! 1 ... 2 ... 3 ... 4 ... 5 ... 6 ... 7 ... 8 ... 9 ... 10!"

The door slides open. Bright light pours on you and all around. Crisp air fills your lungs as you inhale deeply. "Your mind is perfectly alert," I say. "Your thoughts are clear and focused. You are suffused with lightness and energy. When you step out of the elevator, you will be back in your own world, and all through the day you will feel alert, clear, focused, light, energetic. You are at your peak!"

A FEW DOWSING GAMES

When we were children, we learned instinctively by having fun. Too many schoolteachers think fun should be stamped out – I know mine did! I remember next to nothing from those boring lessons, but the silly games where we learned friendship and teamwork in the street with a battered old football ... they're unforgettable. So if you want to expand your mind power and increase your Dowsing Quotient, get a smile on your face with these games.

CRYSTAL HIDE-AND-SEEK

This game helps to strengthen the psychic bond between you and your pendulum. Ask your playing partner to hide an object that is important to you somewhere in your home. Choose something small and laden with memories, such as a photograph of a loved one.

Cup your crystal pendulum in the palm of your hand, let your shoulders relax and your eyelids droop, and focus on that hidden object. Try to transmit the essence of what makes it significant to you, from your brain into the stone. Now open your eyes and breathe deeply: you have reached a state of calm and heightened awareness.

Walk slowly, pulsing images of the object to the crystal. Listen for echoes – when you feel that the stone is reflecting your thoughts, you know that you must be close. Hold your crystal over the places where you think that the object might be hidden. Listen for the instant when the crystal seems to sing in sympathy with the target. At first that note may be faint, but as you practise, the echoes will seem stronger – though the reality is that you are simply getting better at tuning in.

I once played crystal hide-and-seek across a city, racing around Tel Aviv on a bicycle with a chunk of rose quartz in my left hand. It took me just three and a half hours to track down a well-chewed rubber ball that belonged to my beloved dog, Joker!

COLOUR DOWSING

Find three or four identical objects of different colours. Fresh balls of wool are great, or how about painting some eggs (children love this). Put them in matching paper bags, close your eyes and ask someone else to choose one.

Keeping your eyes tightly closed, see if you can divine the colour of the object in the nominated bag. Let the colour energy radiate through your hands and flood your mind. What emotions are you feeling as you handle the object? What colour provokes these emotions? Now hold your pendulum over the object and ask "Are you red?", "Are you green?" and so on, until you get a positive response. At first you'll find the pendulum is right more often than intuition alone, but you'll soon learn to "feel" the colours unaided.

Play the game with friends ... psychic energy always flows best in a group.

NAKED DOWSING

Here's a great game to encourage mental and physical closeness with your partner. Take off your top and close your eyes, then focus on the tingling in your skin while your partner traces a simple shape with his or her hand just a few millimetres away from your back or your tummy. You'll be amazed at how sensitive your skin is to their dowsing energy.

For extra effect, play this game when both of you are totally naked. It's as relaxing as a luxurious massage ... and who knows where it will lead...

Uri's mini-class

Did you know that crystals, like humans, can be left- or right-handed? Immerse your crystal in a glass bowl filled with pure alcohol. A chemist can sell this to you but, if it's difficult to obtain, water will work (although not quite as well!).

Take a bright torch and a pair of polarized sunglasses. Shine the torch through one of the lenses, into the liquid. If the crystal is right-handed, it will glow more intensely; if it's left-handed, its sheen will dull.

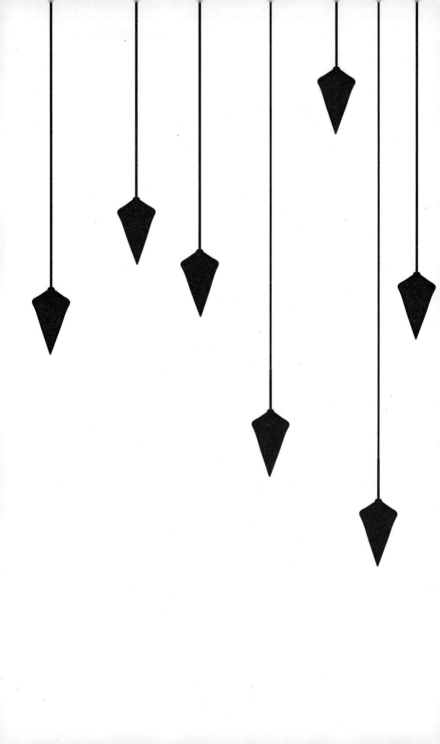

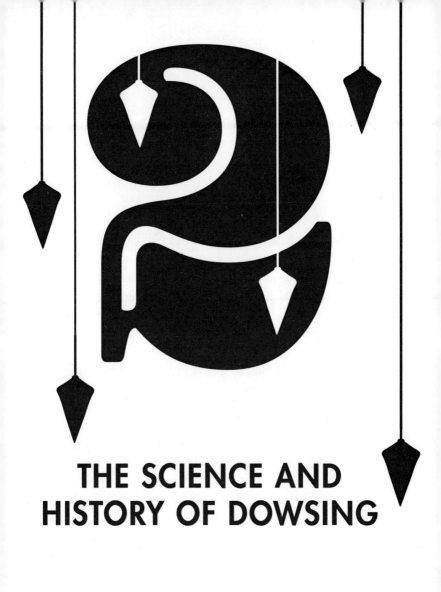

THE SCIENCE AND HISTORY OF DOWSING

SCIENTIFIC EXPLANATIONS OF DOWSING

Whole books have been devoted to the science that underpins dowsing, entire conferences given over to the countless theories and counter-theories that aim to shed light on the mystery. I'm going to give it a couple of pages and I'm being generous, because all the science can be summed up in four simple words: "No one really knows."

Dowsing is like thinking: it happens, even though we can't say how. I've been tested in some of the most prestigious laboratories around the world and I've dowsed for the secret agencies of America, Israel and Mexico. The men in black were as much at a loss as the men in white coats. The paranormal power of the mind is like songwriting ability: put Paul McCartney in a lab and tell him to write another "Yesterday", and he might dry up; but on another day, the creative juices might be flowing.

I believe we place far too much value on scientific explanations. Instead of dissecting our immense potential and examining it under microscopes until we make it vanish, we should embrace it and be thankful.

The best science, on the other hand, can be inspirational. Consider the findings of Professor Hans-Dieter Betz, a physicist at the University of Munich. In a 10-year study, he catalogued German government dowsing projects in Sri Lanka, Zaire, Kenya, Namibia and Yemen, and noted a success rate of 96 per cent. He subsequently estimated the chances of finding water by random drilling should be between 30 and 50 per cent.

Even more impressively, Betz found most dowsers could gauge the depth and quality of the source, and added that many finds were hundreds of feet underground, running in narrow channels – an inaccuracy of a few inches on the surface could mean the drill failed to strike water. "We have established that dowsing works, but have no idea how or why," Betz admitted. "We need to run a lot more tests." He thought dowsers might be able to sense electromagnetic waves generated by flowing water.

Fifty years earlier, Soviet geologists from Moscow State University published research on the "wizard rod", as Russians call it, in the *Journal of Electricity*. The paper kick-started a national programme of dowsing research, with hundreds of Red Army troops joining trials to prove that the forked twig could locate not only water but oil, precious metals and minerals. As dowsing became part of mainstream research in Moscow and Leningrad, a new jargon developed: this was the "biophysical effects method", using "electrophysiological" instruments.

Dr Vincent Reddish, a retired astronomer from the University of Edinburgh, learned to dowse in the Scottish

Highlands and published a paper in *Physics World*, the journal of the UK Institute of Physics. He concluded that his results "may be explained by supposing that linear structures interact with a radiation field to produce standing waves and that these induce a charge on the ground which is conducted through the body".

Amardeo Sarma, a research scientist with Deutsche Telekom, cited the "ideomotor reaction", the impulse that makes an armchair soccer fan twitch his foot when David Beckham rockets the ball past the goalie. "If you think about something or observe something, then you are likely to make small muscular movements in the same direction," he theorized.

It all adds up to this: "No one really knows."

True stories

Retired Cambridge don Tom Lethbridge discovered that all substances have their own dowsing "frequency". A pendulum suspended 11in (28cm) above a sample of oak, for example, spun of its own accord. Over lead, it revolved when the thread was extended to 22in (56cm). Lethbridge also established dowsing frequencies for human emotions, gender and even, he believed, parallel universes.

CELEBRITY DOWSERS

Now that you're a dowser, you're in great company. Nobel-prize-winning scientists, world leaders and bestselling novelists have all been noted dowsers. Leonardo da Vinci, Albert Einstein and Sir Isaac Newton are all said to have been skilled at the craft. The gift is as old as history: Homer wrote of it in both his epic poems, the *Iliad* and the *Odyssey*, and Moses is said, in the Book of Numbers, to have brought water out of desert rocks by striking the ground with his stick.

Four hundred years before Julius Caesar's day, the historian Herodotus recorded how people in Scythia, modern-day Ukraine, dowsed with willow rods

The Queen of Sheba always travelled with dowsers who hunted for gold. Robert Boyle, the founder of modern chemistry, described in 1661 how miners used dowsing rods to discover seams of lead: "One gentleman who employed it declared that it moved without his will, and I saw it bend so strongly as to break in his hand ... those who have seen it may much more readily believe than those who have not." The Frenchman Charles Richet, who won the Nobel prize for medicine, was another scientist who enjoyed demonstrating his dowsing powers.

Dowsers helped to defeat the Nazis in North Africa, and the generals on both sides, Patton and Rommel, were experienced water diviners. Patton gave orders for an entire willow tree to be flown from the USA, to ensure that his troops could always call on dowsers

– their skills were vital, because the Afrika Korps controlled all the oases and were poisoning the wells as they retreated. Without fresh water, the Allied armies would have been doomed in days.

Stephen King, who can describe the supernatural better than anyone, learned to dowse in Maine with his Uncle Clayton. In his book *Danse Macabre*, he writes that "Clayt" could follow a honeybee back to its hive, roll cigarettes one-handed and find water with a wishbone of applewood (birch would do almost as well, but maple would tell lies).

At 12 years old, King was a sceptic: "Uncle Clayt might as well have told me he was going to show me where a flying saucer had landed behind the Methodist meeting hall." After 10 minutes dowsing for a fresh well in front of their house, the boy was a convert – he felt the rod weigh in his hands "as if it were fairly bloated with water". His reaction was to laugh, and that's the healthiest response: dowsing is a wonderful, inexplicable gift, a surprise birthday present on a cosmic scale, well worth a good laugh.

King is happy to leave the science unexplained. His only theory is that if horses can smell water a dozen miles away, why shouldn't humans be able to sense it 98ft (30m) below their feet?

True stories

In 2017 the Central Intelligence Agency (CIA) released files on a series of tests of my abilities conducted by scientists at Stanford Research Institute. In one double-blind experiment they showed me 14 steel cans and asked me to identify which contained a hidden object. I was nervous because I'd never done anything like that before, but I held my hands above the cans and instructed my mind to send energy through them to detect what was inside. I answered correctly in 12 out of the 14 trials – a result the scientists said had a probability of a trillion to one! They concluded that "as a result of Geller's success in this experimental period, we consider that he has demonstrated his paranormal perceptual ability in a convincing and unambiguous manner".

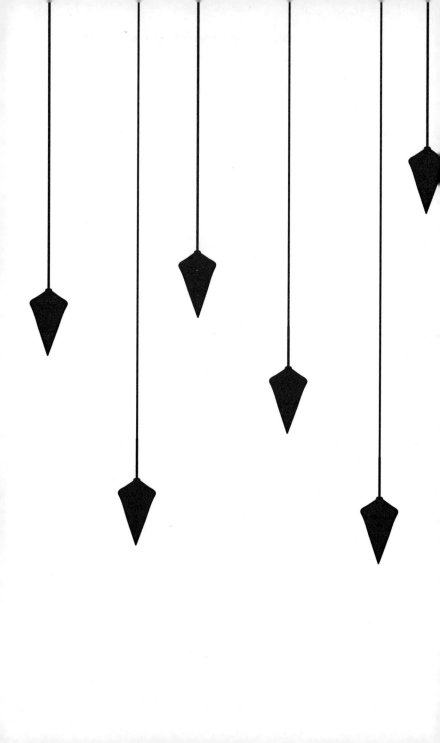

DOWSING FOR
LOST OBJECTS

HOW TO DOWSE THROUGH
YOUR MIND FOR LOST OBJECTS

Everything that's lost wants to be found. This even
applies, believe it or not, to your cellphone. For many
years, I had a simple rule about anything I lost: It's Not
My Fault! Either someone else had done something dumb
and wasn't owning up or the cosmos was conspiring
against me. And it wasn't just car keys that went missing.
The dollars ebbed away, deals collapsed like cardboard
houses and I was losing two things that mattered even
more: my friends and my health. I realized that if I was to
avoid losing my mind, I had to find myself.

   With my whole family, and at the suggestion of
John Lennon (who said I needed to find my spiritual
self), I moved to Japan and for a year lived as simply
as possible, meditating under Mount Fuji in complete
tranquillity. That's where I learned the most important
lesson of my life – to accept responsibility. Blaming other
people is a loser's game.

I still lose things, of course, including my temper from time to time. Few situations are more frustrating than the hold-ups caused by lost objects – usually it's the cellphone, which has become my life-support system. As soon as I remember that I, and only I, have the power to take control of my own life, I'm halfway to finding it again.

First I grip my crystal. The points and edges dig into my hand, an instant indicator of how tense I am about this lost phone. I imagine cool energy thrumming from the stone and into my body, and my grip relaxes. Then I hold the crystal by its thread and say, "Show me 'Yes'". There is a moment of physical release when the stone starts to spin: it's as real as slipping your car key into the ignition and feeling the engine come alive.

I have two key questions: "Is my phone where I left it?" and "Do I want to find it?" The answer to the first is always "Yes" – what else could it be? My wife doesn't go around hiding things, we haven't been burgled, and my dogs are much too clever to need phones. Of course it's where I left it.

The second answer, tellingly, is often "No, you don't want to find your phone." And at a deep, subconscious level, that's true. If I find the phone, I'm connecting to the world, opening my energy to anyone who wants to tap in. And actually, I'd prefer to be back beside the shining waters below Mount Fuji, staring up at the snowline and listening to the rustle of the trees.

Not today. Face the responsibility: this is a day for communication. "I want to find my phone," I say aloud. If I make this statement with enough conviction, the pendulum will start to rotate: "Yes! You do want to find it." And almost always the knowledge will flash in my head as clear and bright as a neon telegram – I've left my phone in the car, or in the conservatory. Or, if I was really trying to lose it, on a plane.

This is a different kind of dowsing. Instead of using the pendulum to track down the external object, I have used it to divine what's going on in my head and my heart.

HOW TO DOWSE THROUGH YOUR HOUSE FOR LOST OBJECTS

When you've lost something around the house and no amount of reciting of affirmations (that is, positive statements: "I want to find it! Yes I do!") can help you to remember where it is, you need to switch to "external" dowsing and use your powers to track down the object. The obvious way is to walk through your rooms with your pendulum, asking, "Is it here?" but this method may not necessarily be the most effective because you're too open to distraction. Your eyes will be darting around, your mind will be probing all the corners that you've already checked twice and your focus will be fractured. Without focus, your dowsing ability will fade.

Retreat to your calm place instead. I have many of these around my home – under the willow by my cascade, inside my glass pyramid, on the riverbank where the barges moor. If your house is hectic, with children or flatmates causing a constant uproar, you must be firm and designate a special place as your sanctuary. A chair beside your bed is a good choice, and the bath is a popular haven ... though it's not ideal to run a bath when you have to find your car keys in a hurry! If things are really crowded, you can always lock yourself in the bathroom, the one place you're guaranteed to get some peace (provided you've switched off your phone).

Say out loud the name of the missing object three times and ask the pendulum, "Is it in this house?" If the answer is positive, ask if it's in that room, and then name the rooms of your home in turn. If you know subconsciously where you left the object, you'll receive a strong response for one of the rooms, but if this is genuinely external dowsing, and your psychic sense is reaching out for something whose location is truly a mystery, you might have to be patient. The pendulum could give you a negative response for every room, so list them aloud again.

When you think you know the room, ask a series of questions to narrow the search. This is a bit like a party game: "Getting hotter! Very hot! Boiling!" Your crystal will tell you when you're hot by swinging in more vigorous, decisive circles when you ask the right questions: "Is it on a shelf? Is it on the floor? Is it in a pocket? Is it in my coat?"

It doesn't matter how improbable the questions become. If all the responses are negative, I'll try silly questions: "Is it under the floorboards? Is it in the oven? Has a dog swallowed it?" Humour is a good way to jog your inspiration: have a laugh and you could suddenly think of the key question to unlock the puzzle.

True stories

Former US president Jimmy Carter revealed to
university students that the CIA had consulted
a remote viewer. When spy satellites failed
to track down a missing US plane that had
crashed in the Central African Republic, the
director of the Central Intelligence Agency
(CIA) contacted a woman from California who
"went into a trance and gave some latitude
and longitude figures. We focused our satellite
cameras on that point and the plane was there."

HOW I LEARNED TO DOWSE WITH A MAP

Here's where the real magic begins …
If I could explain what makes map-dowsing work,
I'd win a Nobel prize. I'd be Professor Sir Uri Geller,
or Lord Geller of Spoon. Then again, as I know that
doing something like that could well cause the magic
to evaporate, before too long my catchphrase might
change from "Can you see it bending?" to "Do you
want fries with that?"

Read on with your mind, and probably your mouth,
wide open. You may feel science can explain why
the pendulum swings or the forked stick twitches,
but no kind of current science explains why I am
able to detect water, minerals and even lost objects

as surely with a map, at a desk in my own home,
as I am on the ground. When I hold my left hand
above a detailed map and visualize, for example,
a reservoir of untapped oil, my skin tingles over the
precise coordinates that designate a place, maybe
thousands of miles away, where oil lies hidden. If I
push my forefinger down toward the spot, I feel springy
resistance, as if I were pointing through jelly.

You may find this impossible to believe. All I can
say is: look at my home. That's the proof. I bought
my mansion by the Thames for £1 million in the mid
1980s, long after my heyday as a paranormal TV star.
The money from the days of hanging out in New York
with John Lennon and Jackie O was gone, wasted
in sprees that were as addictive and destructive as
my food obsessions. What saved my career was the
extraordinary discovery that a map beneath my hand
had the same effect on my psychic senses as a billion
tons of rock.

I owe all this to Sir Val Duncan, who was chairman
of Rio Tinto-Zinc Corporation when I met him at a party
in London in 1973. "How much longer are you going
to run around the world performing for audiences?"
he asked. "Don't you want to start making some real
money?" Sir Val invited me to his home in Majorca and
set me a test. "In one of these rooms my gold wedding
ring is hidden," he challenged. "Find it!"

That was easy. I'd been playing the game since I
was a child. But then he produced a blueprint of the
house, hid the ring again, and asked me to locate

it using just the map. When my hand hovered over the corner of the dressing room where the ring was lurking, in a pile of towels, Sir Val clapped me on the shoulder and roared with laughter. "Your talent is going to make us both a lot of money," he said.

Sadly, Sir Val died soon afterwards, at just 62. He didn't live to see it, but the gift he had awakened in me bloomed: it took me gold prospecting in Africa, oil-hunting in Mexico, diving for treasure in the Bermuda Triangle and even searching for buried Nazi gemstones.

HOW YOU CAN LEARN TO
DOWSE WITH A MAP

When I went gold prospecting in the South Seas in 1985, the multinational that hired me laid on a plane to criss-cross the Solomon Islands. I rode at about 3,000ft (914m), one hand held out like a third wing, and imagined the dense yellow sparkle of hidden ore, emanating like sunlight. When its rays hit my palm, it was as if I had put my hand close to an oven. "It's down there," I yelled, "right below us," and the navigator marked the coordinates, at Guadalcanal. The same technique led me to a strike in Brazil, among many other far-flung places.

That's hard work, though rewarding. You can charter your own psychic plane by taking a thin sheet of Plexiglas® and dividing it into a grid with a marker pen, like a giant game of noughts and crosses. Down the left of the grid, label the rows with letters – A, B, C … Across the bottom, mark the columns with numbers 1, 2, 3 … Lay the grid over your map, hold your pendulum and focus your eyes on the A1 square. Remember to ask the crystal to "Show me 'Yes'" before you start dowsing, just to get yourself in tune. Now visualize what you want to find – a hoard of historic coins, for example. Make the picture as clear as you can in your mind, and ask, "Is it here, in A1?"

If you're the methodical type, you can work right through the grid. I'm more scattershot: I start with any square that attracts my inner eye. To get a feel for likely places, run your palm about an inch (2.5cm) above the grid. You're looking for any sensation – heat, tickling or a rubbery resistance.

True stories

I was delighted when the seven-year-old son of a good friend won the "buried treasure" at his school fête. He had to mark an "X" on the pirates' map where he believed the loot to be hidden. Result: five £1 coins and a box of beads. Not a bad haul, me hearties!

"I did it just the way you showed me, Uri," the lad told me over the phone. "I held my palm over the map and I moved it slowly. Where it felt hot and tingly, I put my cross. My friends thought I was silly, because it was in the water, off the edge of the island."

"Maybe the pirates threw their plunder overboard," I suggested.

STRIKE IT RICH

Get hold of some detailed topographic maps (such as Ordnance Survey in the UK) and you can try prospecting for precious metals and minerals wherever you may be. Here are just a few hotspots:

Gold – Dolgellau, Gwynedd; the Spanish Peaks, Colorado

Sapphire – Carbis Bay, St Ives, Cornwall; Helena Valley, Montana

Opal – Okehampton, Devon; Yowah, Queensland, Australia

Topaz – St Austell, Cornwall

Turquoise – Caldbeck Fells, Cumbria

Amethyst – Matlock, Derbyshire; Thunder Bay, Ontario, Canada

Rock crystal – Clifton, Bristol; Miller Mountain, Arkansas

Ruby – Franklin, North Carolina

Amateur treasure-hunter Brian Grove believes untold riches are scattered around Britain, waiting to reward anyone with a spade and the right intuition. "Billions of pounds' worth of treasure is buried just beneath your feet," he says. "This includes coins, figurines and chalices, jewels with royal connections, gold nuggets, pirate treasure, and tools and weapons, in some cases worth tens or even hundreds of thousands – all waiting for someone to dig them up." He is enthusiastic about gold, which has been found in every British county except East Lothian and Renfrew in Scotland.

True stories

Usually I dowse with my hands, but recently I was standing in the middle of the construction site of the new Uri Geller Museum in Old Jaffa when I felt a familiar tingling sensation coming through my feet. Convinced that there was something buried in the rubble beneath me, I contacted the Israel Antiquities Authority, who came to supervise the dig. Lo and behold, we soon came upon the ruins of an olive oil soap factory that could date back hundreds of years before the Ottoman Empire. I stretched my arms out and began to dowse, thinking we would uncover ancient coins down there, but instead I located a water jug, a bronze strainer and – an archaeological first for Israel – a clog carved from a palm tree.

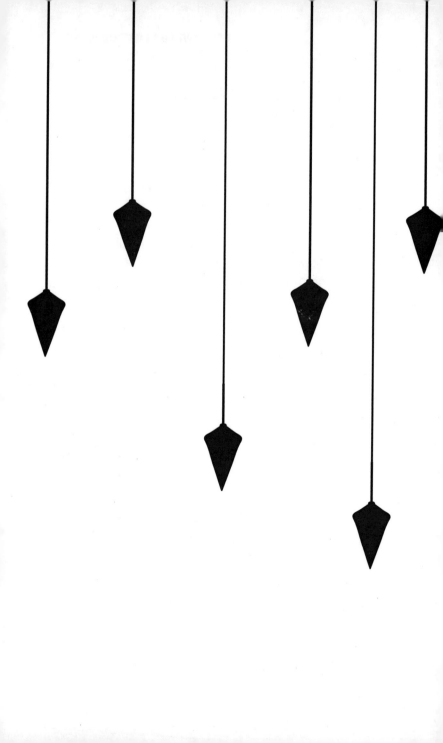

RECAPTURE JOY
WITH DOWSING

LOVE AND LIGHT-HEARTED GAMES

We're all looking for love. Psychologists tell me I am searching for it every time I step out on stage. I'm blessed with a wonderful family, but my father was a hard man to please and he left my mother when I was a boy. Perhaps when I perform I am seeking the adoration my dad never showed me. Or perhaps I am leaning too heavily on the theories of my forebear, Sigmund Freud!

One thing is certain: I love to entertain. Many times I have been tempted to turn my back on the cameras and the crowds, to become a scientific researcher, a spy, a politician or an agent, but my heart keeps pulling me back. "Follow your bliss," said Joseph Campbell, the philosopher who believed ancient myths could teach us the path to happiness and fulfilment. Do what you love doing most.

What the heart knows, the brain often obscures. It's impossible to think your way through an emotional tangle.

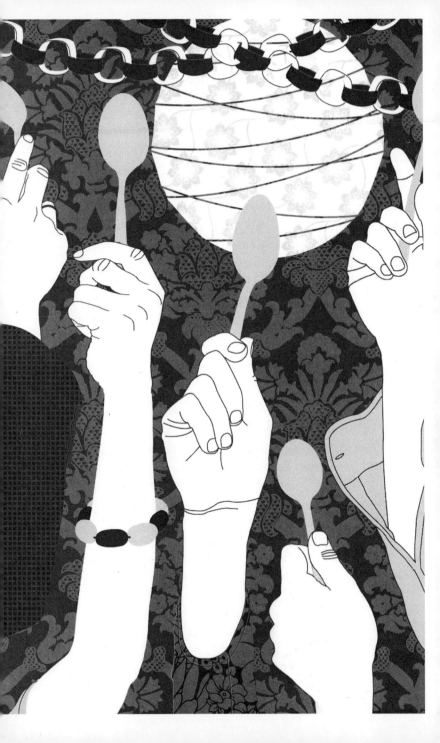

But your pendulum can show you the way. When you long to "follow your bliss" but you can't tell which way the path lies, take out your crystal and start asking questions.

Focus on your emotional doubts. Don't be afraid to ask the hard questions: nothing about love is easy. "Can I trust this person? Does this person trust me? Should I take the risk? Are we right for each other? Can we make it right?" If it is hard to frame the questions, just hold your pendulum – it might start to swing, responding to a question in your heart for which you can't find words.

I've said it already and I'll say it again: we learn fastest, and dowse best, when we're having fun. Teach your friends to use the pendulum and try these party games!

TRUTH OR DARE

In this classic game, players take turns to decide whether they want to answer an embarrassing question ("truth") or perform a ridiculous or risqué stunt ("dare"). In my version, which focuses on the "truth" element of the game, you're allowed to lie if the questions get too uncomfortable – but everyone else is holding a pendulum and can dowse to find out if you're telling the truth. I've found the only way to succeed in this game is to think like a politician and give truthful answers that sidestep the question. An outright lie will be found out!

QUEEN OF HEARTS

Take the 13 heart cards from a pack, shuffle and lay
them out face down in a circle. One person, the thief,
removes each card in turn and asks, "Have I stolen the
queen of hearts away?" The other players hold their
pendulums. When your crystal starts to swing, cry, "Queen
of hearts!" and the thief must show the card. If you're
right, you become the thief; if you're wrong, you're out.
Inexperienced dowsers might find that one pendulum will
set the others swinging. Suggestion is a powerful force.

BERLIN WALL

Ask your friends to imagine that an invisible wall is
dividing the room. Leave the room, or shut your eyes and
cover your ears, while they decide on the location of the
wall. You can't see it and you don't know where it is, so
ask your pendulum. Holding the bobber a few inches in
front of your stomach, walk slowly around the room and
ask your pendulum out loud, "Is the wall here?" You'll
probably get no answer until, suddenly, the pendulum
starts swinging. You've just crossed the invisible divide.

ENHANCE YOUR CHILDLIKE MIND
... AND BEND SPOONS

Dowsing and spoon-bending are powers that draw on
the same parts of our brain, the unmapped 90 per cent
that we don't use during conscious thought. As your

psychic gifts develop in one area, you will become more confident about tuning in to the rest of your mind power. I call it the art of intuitive living, where you learn to listen to your instincts.

My friend Desmond Morris, the anthropologist and veteran TV presenter whose bestsellers include *The Naked Ape*, believes my metal-bending gift could be directly connected to the homing instinct that enables animals to trek halfway around the world and find the nesting sites and mating grounds that their ancestors have used for millennia. Birds migrate, salmon swim upriver, turtles cross oceans, and they all do it without the benefit of GPS (Global Positioning System). Are they attuned to the Earth's magnetic forces, ponders Desmond – and am I using the same receptors to bend metal?

"In terms of evolution, where is the practical benefit of metal-bending?" he asked me. "Mankind has been working with metal tools for only a few thousand years. In evolution, that's no time at all. But dowsing and path-finding – those skills could spell the difference between survival and extinction."

He asked me to take off my socks and bend a spoon with my toes. No one has ever asked that before – more proof of what a dramatically original thinker my friend is. (In case you're wondering, the spoon bent like butter over a burning match.)

If you want to learn how to bend a spoon (with your hands, not your feet), it's easy. You need three things: an open mind, a spoon … and a sense of fun. Anyone can do it, but you might not have much luck if you sit there scowling at your cutlery like you're trying to hypnotize it ... spoons don't hypnotize well. The best method is to throw a party. Get at least a dozen friends together, and pick the kind of people who'll try anything for a laugh, because your efforts won't be helped if there's a moaning sceptic around. And invite people who have children: kids make great spoon-benders and their happy energy is infectious.

Let everyone choose a spoon or a fork from a basket of cutlery. When you pick your piece, ask it out loud, "Will you bend for me?" If you feel a sympathetic tingle in your fingertips, this is the one for you. Use your dowser's instinct.

Tell your guests to hold up their spoons and shout, "Bend! Bend!" The atmosphere now will be hilarious – ideal conditions for parascientific phenomena. You're about as far removed from dry laboratory experiments as possible. Holding your spoon by the bowl, rub the stem between your forefinger and thumb. Tell it to bend, bend, bend! Walk around and tell your friends' cutlery to bend – especially encourage the children.

Often, particularly for first-time party-goers, nothing will happen for a few minutes – and then one spoon will start bending. Usually it begins with the children, most commonly the girls. I think complete innocent open-mindedness is the key. And once one bends, a chain reaction kicks in. Everybody begins to believe that metal-bending is possible for anyone. You'll all be tying knots in knives and loops in ladles – have fun!

HOW TO TELL THE GENDER
OF AN UNBORN CHILD

An unborn child is a powerful trigger to our intuition. The greatest feeling in the world for a couple is when a baby kicks and turns in the womb. The days when Hanna was expecting our children, Daniel and Natalie, were some of the happiest in my life, and we didn't need ultrasound scans to be sure that the first one was a boy, the second a girl.

It's traditional in so many cultures worldwide to discover the gender of an unborn baby by dowsing that this technique is accepted as more than just an old wives' tale. Hold a pendulum above the mother-to-be's left palm, and watch which way the weight swings – clockwise for a girl, anticlockwise or back and forth for a boy. To make certain, ask your pendulum aloud, "Is this a girl?" and you'll get a yes or no answer. Unless, of course, it's twins!

Many people will tell you the pendulum must be a wedding ring on a thread, but any dowsing pendulum will work.

It's fascinating that folklore rules that the pendulum must be held over the mother's hand and not her belly. Our hands are most sensitive to the energy flowing around our body: our palms don't only pick up dowsing signals, they reflect them too. That's why psychics like to stare at your palm when they predict your future (trade secret: the lines are irrelevant, it's the aura that counts!). Someone who has never used a pendulum before is more likely to pick up an accurate reading over the palm.

Uri's mini-class

Am I going too quickly for you? If you're still getting to grips with basic dowsing, this exercise will help you hone your abilities. You'll need six cups and saucers. Ask a friend to pour an inch (2.5cm) of water into one, place a saucer on top of each cup so you can't see what's inside, then arrange them on a table. Hold your pendulum over each in turn and ask: "Is there water in this cup?" To vary the test, put water in five and see if your dowsing power can find the empty one.

Hold your pendulum over each cup in turn and ask:
"Is there water in this cup?"

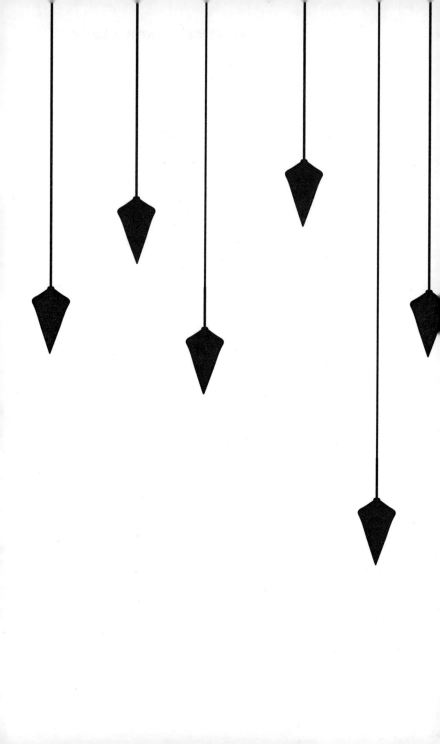

5

DOWSING
FOR SUCCESS

MY MEXICO ADVENTURE

Every psychic power has its dark side. The dark side of dowsing is greed. I learned this in Mexico, when I helped the government discover oil fields worth untold billions. I could have made myself a vast fortune. I could also have got a bullet in my head.

I was living in Mexico City, the guest of the president's wife. Her name was Señora Carmen Romana de López Portillo – I called her Muncy, and my powers fascinated her. She lavished gifts on me, and I demonstrated my own gifts to her friends. Today I would be ashamed to live that way, but in 1976 I was happy to be a pampered psychic pet. Muncy's idea of a fun shopping trip was to take me to a warehouse packed with antiques, luxury goods and jewellery. She opened a box and told me to take whatever I touched. The box was full of watches: the top layer was diamond-studded Rolexes, but I reached deeper and pulled out a Vacheron Constantin, worth half as much again.

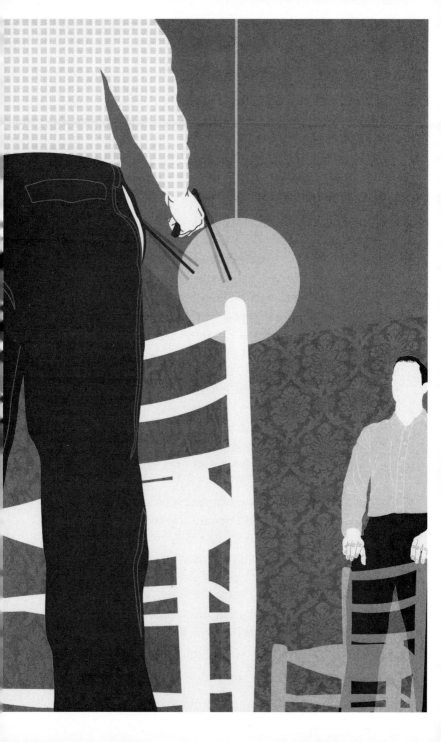

I was overcome with the wealth that was there for the taking, and I seldom gave a thought to the immense poverty that was all around in Mexico. At one of Muncy's parties, I met Jorge Dias Serrano, director general of Petróleos Mexicanos, who challenged me to dowse for oil. The first experiment was in the presidential offices, where I found a tiny phial, buried within a flowerpot. Serrano was amazed, and invited me to inspect several possible drilling sites, first by dowsing over maps, then on helicopter fly-overs.

I didn't demand a percentage, because I was simply having fun. That probably saved my life. As a reward for my dowsing, I was given a Mexican passport in the name of Uri Geller-Freud. I was made a treasury agent, which gave me a licence to swagger with jewel-studded silver pistols at my hip or in holsters at my shoulders, and to fly in and out of the States as often as I wished, with full diplomatic privileges – no one searched me and I could carry what I liked. I was given a golden ticket on AeroMéxico – free flights wherever I wanted, whenever I wanted. If a flight was full, I sat with the pilots. If a flight was about to leave, it got held until I was aboard. Nobody but the president of the airline and the president of the country possessed golden tickets, and Muncy had to push hard to get me into the club.

However, after scandalous (and untrue) stories started to circulate about my friendship with Muncy, I had to leave the country in a hurry. All I took with me was my passport … and my life. Sitting in my New York apartment months later, I saw a *Wall Street Journal* report

.that described the biggest ever oil strike in the Gulf of Mexico – precisely where my dowsing had predicted.

It was a lesson I have never forgotten: dowse for fun and not for greed. I believe that our minds have an innate sense of balance, and when our actions threaten to topple that equilibrium, alarm bells clang and sirens shrill. Most of us are very good at ignoring those warnings ... learn to listen for yours.

True stories

Alfred Wegener, the German geologist who shocked the scientific world with his theory that the continents were drifting on the Earth's surface, was a dowser. He once mapped a fault in the Earth's crust with a pendulum, while riding on the back of a yak in Russia's Ural mountains.

DOWSING YOUR INTUITION

I speak three languages, but sometimes I am lost for words. Mostly, I think in English, but we often speak Hebrew at home. With my mother I usually spoke Hungarian, which is also a great language for swearing: I use it to let off steam.

But every now and then, I can't find the word I need.

My brain knows it, but it won't release the information. It's "on the tip of my tongue", hovering on the borders of my subconscious mind. Our intuitive sense works in the same way. It is constantly trying to send information that often cannot quite make contact with our conscious thoughts. Dowsing makes the connection. It illuminates the thought paths the way ultraviolet light makes a thread of white cotton glow like neon.

Those paths can lead you to success. To find them takes study, practice and patience, but if you set out on this journey you can be confident the paths will take you to wonderful places. Time spent dowsing is always worthwhile: it hones your intuition. The emphasis on science in Western culture means we glorify the rational and the logical, forgetting that most of our decisions are based on emotions and feelings. Human beings are not computers. Emotions are not mathematical equations.

Dowsing is the surest tool for deciphering our half-formed thoughts and feelings. Pick up your pendulum and interrogate your heart. Ask any questions that pop into your mind: it's impossible to ask the wrong thing. This isn't a job interview – it's something much more important. This is your life. When you first start dowsing, you're like a musician learning an instrument: all the talent is inside you, but you have to reach it and free it with patience and practice.

Trust your instincts. Learn to listen to them with the pendulum, and respect their power. How many times do you hear of people who avoided road accidents because they yielded to an impulse to take a different route, or who escaped a plane or rail crash because they felt a sudden, irrational fear of taking that connection? These stories appear every time there's a major disaster in the news. And how many people have died because, tragically, they heard the voice of intuition and dismissed it as irrational?

Our instincts have evolved to protect our lives. Take hold of your pendulum and tune in.

DIVING IN THE BERMUDA TRIANGLE

Perhaps the greatest dowsing adventure of my life was an expedition to discover Atlantis with the explorer Ambrogio Fogar. We scuba-dived in the Bermuda Triangle, off Bimini, where Fogar challenged me to bend a spoon underwater. The results were mind-blowing.

Fogar was an intrepid yachtsman who had become the first Italian to sail westward around the world solo. Fascinated by legends of an ancient world that sank into the Atlantic, and with newspaper headlines screaming about ships and aeroplanes that vanished off the radar in a mysterious stretch of water around Bermuda, he contacted me in New York to invite me on a Boy's Own mission: to search for a lost world. The psychic Edgar Cayce had long ago predicted that Atlantis would be discovered in these waters. But it had also been confidently sited in the Mediterranean, the Indian Ocean and under the Antarctic ice floes.

I had doubts – I didn't want to cap my career as an international man of mystery by disappearing in the

Bermuda Triangle – but Fogar radiated confidence. He was fresh from a transatlantic race, which he'd tackled in a catamaran called *Surprise*. The surprise was that there was no cabin: Fogar slept in a crate in one of the hulls. I decided that anyone who could do something that mad simply had to be sane, so I flew to Hamilton, Bermuda.

I had never tried dowsing underwater. I wish I had: my dives with Fogar made me realize what I had been missing, because I found my dowsing gifts were amplified underwater.

Swimming in 120ft (37m) of water over the Bimini Wall, a reef that Fogar believed could have been human-made, I felt empowered, as if my body was plugged into 10,000 volts of psychic energy. The vast tracts of water surrounding me enhanced my ability, and I felt as though I was shining X-rays on the ocean bed. Again and again I was able to point to structures looming from the sea floor that seemed to be the ruins of a city – yet despite the many reports of planes and ships that had sunk here I could find no wrecks.

On one dive Fogar handed me a thick-stemmed spoon. It shattered as soon as I began to stroke it, not merely snapping but dissolving into fragments. I have never seen that happen, before or since. We both felt that this was a natural vortex, a black hole in the ocean that could break metal as if it were porcelain, and our fears turned to our oxygen tanks: if the aqualungs fragmented, we would be blown to shreds. Reluctantly, we called off the expedition, both of us believing that an ancient city, perhaps even Atlantis, had collapsed into

the sea here. Whether it was the cause or the victim of the vortex, we'll never know.

PSI-TRACKING, AND HOW TO UNCOVER ARCHAEOLOGICAL REMAINS AND FOSSILS

When Göte Andersson asked his father, Arthur, a keen diviner, if his dowsing rod could detect the human aura, the older man was sceptical. A talent for finding water doesn't automatically make you a believer in poltergeists, UFOs or fairies at the bottom of the garden, and Arthur expressed his doubts loudly.

Undeterred, Göte stood 12ft (3.7m) from a chair
and attempted to project his body's energy field by
imagining that he was gripping the back of the chair
with his hands. Arthur held his dowsing rod over the
chair and gaped in astonishment as its tip twitched.

More remarkable still, Arthur found the stick reacted
all along the path from the chair to his son, as if a
stream of energy ran through an invisible cable in the
air. The two men experimented and found the rod could
trace a line wherever Göte focused his mind – almost
as if it could detect his thoughts.

This was in Värmland in Sweden, in 1987, and
Göte conducted hundreds of tests with every dowser
he could contact. His work, which won Sweden's Imich
Project Prize in 1994, the psychical-research equivalent
of the Nobel prize, proved the existence of what Göte
calls "psi-tracks": the mental chains that connect our
brains to the objects we are visualizing. The power of
psi-tracking has dramatic implications, as Göte showed
when he and his father helped to catch a bank robber.
Security cameras had captured a vivid portrait of one
gang member during a hold-up at a bank in Nysäter
in September 1991, and the image was published in
newspapers. Göte focused on the photo in the garden of
his father's home, while Arthur dowsed the path of his psi-
track, the mental path that connected him to the criminal.

The pair marked the track with sticks and repeated
the experiment in another town. Charting the psi-tracks
on a map, they saw the trails crossed in a town called
Arvika, more than 40 miles (64km) north. Göte called

the police and, after an investigation, the robber was arrested in Arvika.

I wouldn't advise you to start chasing bank robbers, but I do recommend that you explore the potential of psi-tracking. Ask your partner to sit in the centre of a room, close his or her eyes and focus on an object without telling you what it is. Dowse all around, looking for the psi-track – I visualize it as a twisting, multicoloured cord of liquid flowing from the mind's eye. When your rods are in or over the track, they should twitch. This may take plenty of practice, so be patient – you'll soon be able to identify the focal object with confidence. This makes a fantastic party game, by the way, because your partner doesn't have to know anything about dowsing, so long as the game is played with an open mind. You'll look like a wizard of a mind-reader!

Some people are able to see the psi-track, especially if they also see glimpses of the human aura. It's a rare talent, though, unlike dowsing.

Use psi-tracking to find fossils, archaeological remains, rare crystals and even buried treasure when you're out prospecting. Your rods are much better than a metal detector. If you find a Viking brooch or a hoard of Roman coins, I'd love to hear about it.

True stories

Israeli general Moshe Dayan, a keen antiquarian, asked me to dowse for ancient artefacts for his collection. We regularly visited the beaches at Ashdod, Ashkelon and Caesarea in his jeep in the middle of the night and I always found something interesting: ancient lamps, coins and ceramics decorated with etchings. Usually artefacts are given to the Israel Antiquities Authority, but I believe that Dayan displayed them in his garden.

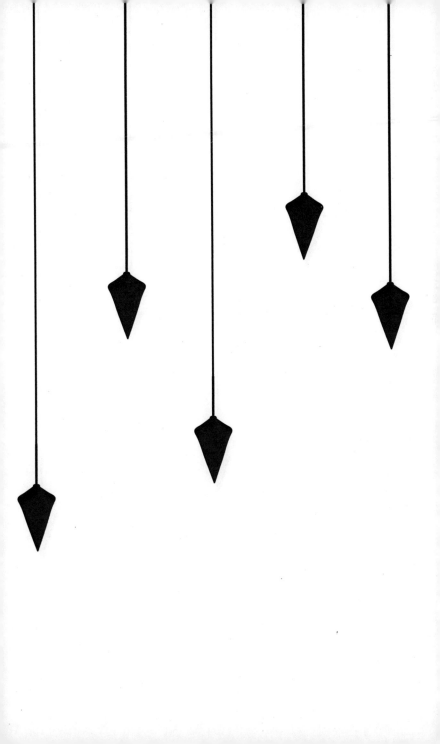

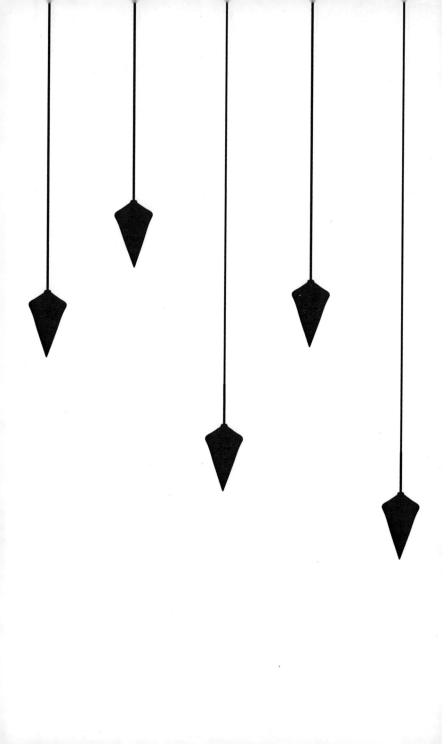

DOWSING FOR
HEALTH AND
WELLBEING

BODY DOWSING – READING HEALTH SIGNS

Your pendulum is a psychic thermometer: it measures your psi energy, like a nurse taking your temperature. When your psi-power is at its peak, you'll see a strong reaction from the crystal – it will respond almost instantly to your questions, even when you ask silently, and it will swing in confident arcs and circles. When my spirits are up, my pendulum becomes positively exuberant.

When you're low, your pendulum will be sluggish. Dowsing power isn't a constant: it ebbs and flows with your mood, your physical health and your internal clock. I'm never at my best after a heavy meal. On the other hand, a swift shower sets my energy levels zinging – three minutes of hot water blasting in my face and ... cutlery, watch out!

Alcohol leaves residues in your body that damp down your psi. If you drink wine every day, you're throwing a blanket over your potential. It's not only your pendulum that will suffer – a drinker's dreams are fragmented and muted, because booze cuts the connection to the deepest levels of the subconscious.

Regular drinkers should try this experiment: put a notebook by your bed and, if you wake in the night, jot down a few words that spring from your dreams. You don't have to write an essay – a handful of adjectives might capture the dream's essence. Chances are, though, that if you're going to bed after half a bottle of Burgundy every night, the only adjectives that matter will be "boring" and "flat". Try going teetotal for a day or two and witness the difference. I'm lucky – though hard drinkers are commonplace in the entertainment industry, I share a genetic quirk with about 25 per cent of Jewish men that makes it impossible for me to tolerate alcohol. Even half a glass of champers and I fall over.

Here's a great exercise to prove that your mind can project energy to influence everything around you.

- Light a candle and place it in a holder on the floor. Kneel or sit several feet away. It's important to be comfortable, with your back straight. Make sure there's no draught and that your breathing cannot make the flame flicker.

- Focus on the light. You are going to make it move with the power of your mind.

- Visualize the flame leaning to the right. Silently command it: "Move to the right." Feel your energy as a weight, gently pressing on the flame until it bows.

- Now let the thought go. Let your mind clear – a

simple technique is to visualize a cloudless sky. The flame will return to upright.

I find this exercise relaxing and uplifting – it affirms my psychic power. The more you do it, the easier it gets.

DOWSING FOR ALLERGIES

Our intuition knows what's good for us. Our conscious mind often doesn't – that's why we make so many bad decisions. Smoking is a good example. It's an addiction; but it's also a conscious decision, because it's impossible to buy a packet of cigarettes when you're asleep. If instinct were king, no one would smoke. It's as counter-intuitive to light up a cigarette as it is to jump in front of a bus. But our instincts are easily overruled by our brains.

Much of what we eat is bad for us: high in fat, high in sugar, high in artificial additives. But for some, bad foods can be even more destructive – they can trigger deadly allergic reactions. Anaphylactic shock, a sometimes fatal condition sparked by nuts, bee stings and other causes, is becoming widespread. But lesser allergies are also on the rise, and if you're suffering from mood swings, headaches, mild depression or constant tiredness, you could benefit from cutting out certain foods.

Trial and error might identify your allergy, but your pendulum could streamline the process. Dowse to discover what you should cut from your diet. Start with the obvious question: "Am I allergic to any foodstuff?"

Your intuition will know the answer. You could make a list of everything you regularly eat, and ask about each item in turn. Am I allergic to bread? Am I allergic to cornflakes? Another method is to make broader inquiries. Do I buy my allergen from the supermarket? Does it come in a packet? Does it come in a bottle? Is it a glass bottle? Is it a plastic bottle?

The best method is to hold your pendulum over a portion of food and ask: "Does this food cause an allergic reaction in me?" Hold the food in one hand as you dowse or, if it's too messy (like jam or wine), put some on a plate or in a glass and bring one hand close to it. If you get a positive reaction, try dowsing over different amounts: a pat of butter might elicit a strong response, while a scraping gets nothing. Maybe the problem isn't allergy but over-indulgence!

Some things, such as sugary drinks, may not be actively damaging, but they aren't too healthy either. Your pendulum can be an accurate gauge. Here's a test that always impresses children. Pour a fizzy drink and ask, "Is this drink bad for Jimmy?" If the pendulum signals "No", Jimmy's going to be delighted.

But now you ask, "On a scale of 1 to 20, how healthy is this drink for Jimmy? 1, 2, 3?" Your pendulum will signal "Yes" until, at a certain number, it switches to "No". And if that drink scores only 4 out of 20, while a glass of apple juice rates 18, Jimmy will see why he can't guzzle pop all the time.

The counted scale is also a good way to gauge how fresh food is: "On a scale of 1 to 20, is this apple fresh? 1, 2, 3 ..." Try it on a freshly picked fruit and then with a shrink-wrapped apple from the other side of the world – you'll be horrified.

In no way, shape or form, though, am I telling any of my readers to abandon conventional medicine. On the contrary, I advise that you have a thorough medical check-up every year and consult your doctor about any concerns you have. When sick children visit my home, I teach them to be positive thinkers, to believe in themselves and to be motivated and inspired to get well. Of course, all this is in parallel to conventional medicine.

PSYCHIC GARDENING

Many dowsers believe that the force that guides them
is the same energy that flows through healers. It's an
attractive theory, though I am not a healer myself: I believe
that my powers make me a catalyst to trigger healing and
regenerative power in other people. I love to see the faces
of children who visit my home from hospitals and hospices
when they watch a key bend or a seed sprout in my hand.
"There's no limit to what you can do with your mind," I tell
them, "if you have faith in its power."

There's a beautiful bush in my garden, a hibiscus,
which explodes in magnificent purple blooms. One
day my gardener, Joe, challenged me to change the
colour: "That'd make you a great TV show ... *The Psychic
Gardener!*" I closed my fist around a bud and imagined
searing light streaming into the molecules of the plant,
filling it with all the colours of the prism. Two weeks
later, a shocked Joe led me outside to see the hibiscus
in flower: amid all the purple blossoms, there was one
shimmering white bloom.

You can experiment with your own psychic gardening
by taking two small pot plants – ivy and spider plants are
both good – and holding your pendulum over each in
turn. Above one, focus positive thoughts that will set your
pendulum spinning in its "Yes" trajectory. Visualize the plant
erupting in leaves and greenery, in a liquid pool of light.
With the other, imagine a wintry landscape where the
plant is in hibernation. Tell it, "Stay safe but don't grow,"
and your pendulum will trace its "No" path. Measure the

progress of each plant and prepare to be amazed at their different rates of growth.

You could try focusing seriously negative thoughts at the plant, but I believe fervently that it's dangerous to summon up anger and hatred, even for an experiment. Many pagans believe in the threefold law – if you wish harm to others, it will come back three times as horribly on you. Your plants are as much a part of the universal life force as you are, so be sure to respect them: order one to hibernate, but don't hurt it.

The weirdest paranormal experiment ever was conducted by an ex-CIA interrogator named Cleve Backster who pioneered polygraphs, the lie detectors that home in on human stress levels by measuring changes in the flow of electricity through skin.

Backster connected his potted rubber plant to a lie detector to see if the needle flickered when the plant was harmed. There was no reaction when he dipped a leaf in hot coffee – maybe rubber plants like a good, frothy cappuccino – but when he thought to himself, "I'm going to light a match and burn a stem," the polygraph went into overdrive.

Plants, it seems, can read our minds. Backster went on to prove that his plant shared in the suffering of even the tiniest creatures, by watching the needle jump every time he dropped a live shrimp into boiling water.

I told you it was weird.

Uri's mini-class

To relax your mind before dowsing, use this simple meditation. Repeat to yourself, "A cool breeze is blowing on my forehead." Between each repetition take a deep breath and let it out slowly. When you have recited the mantra six or eight times, say once, "My mind is calm."

DOWSING FOR EARTH ENERGY

Carry your crystal with you all the time and you'll soon find there are places where it seems almost alive with energy. You'll be conscious of it, thrumming in your bag or your pocket. I always carry crystals, and I know they become supercharged at hotspots on the Earth's surface where energy is focused. These places aren't hard to find, as wise humans will have been tapping into the energy source for millennia. Stonehenge is one of the most outstanding examples, and you'll find stone circles all over the world – take out your pendulum at the centre of one and ask it, "Is this a place of power?" It will spin like a helicopter blade!

Some dowsers believe these hotspots are connected by invisible lines that carry current like electricity on a web. They call them ley lines, and if you're sensitive to them you'll be fascinated to explore their intersections and lattices with your dowsing rods. The pyramids of Giza stand at the hub of a spider's web of ley lines; so do the ruins of Machu Picchu, the ancient Inca temple of Peru. My home is built on the site of a 1,000-year-old healing centre, and many visitors have commented how an hour in the gardens here is as revitalizing as a week's holiday.

You don't have to travel to the pyramids or Peru to find your own hotspot. Energy will branch off the ley lines and flow straight to you if you invite it. You'll need to be in a favourite place, one you can visit at any time. It might be your own room if you feel calm and protected there, or a place of worship, a peaceful nook in a park or even a cosy corner of a coffee bar. Ultimately, it's a place in your mind, and I've talked with prisoners who say that meditation, yoga or Buddhism has enabled them to discover a mental haven that's more real than their cell.

If you're tired or ill when you go to find this special spot, hold your pendulum and ask: "Am I in the right place to let the energy of the Earth begin to heal me?"

When you see a positive response, hold your crystal and imagine trickles of light running like beads of mercury and swelling into a shining pool around you. The light leaps up to strike wherever it's most needed: if your head aches, if your joints hurt, the light pours in and flushes out the pain. Imagine yourself floating in a luminous ball.

As well as attracting energy, you can direct it. When problems occur in a specific place, such as your bedroom, use your dowsing tool to investigate.

If you're having trouble sleeping or you have sexual difficulties, ask if the bed itself is the problem. Perhaps it's facing the wrong way or it's placed opposite a door, which might make you feel vulnerable and self-conscious. Keep asking questions: with the right question comes the answer.

I've helped many athletes, including Formula 1 racing drivers and Premiership footballers, tune in to their intuition to avoid injuries. Dowsing is a great tool for listening to your body – if an athlete is doing something in training that puts unnecessary stress on a joint or muscle, the subconscious is always the first to know.

True stories

Dowser Christopher Strong, who has a degree in natural sciences from Cambridge University, warns that water deep beneath the foundations of a house can set up strange and uncomfortable vibes. "Underground water generates electromagnetic energy at a frequency which is incompatible with the human body," he says. "This can weaken the immune system and, in many cases, people can become ill or depressed. When people mention how a property feels, they are often picking up subconsciously on this."

Uri's mini-class

A favourite meditation is designed to burn away any negative energy that we've brought into the house without meaning to. I am not always a patient man and, when all the telephones are ringing at once and I'm late for a show, I get short-tempered. Even the dogs hide from me!

My outbursts of irritation are always short-lived, but intense emotions are less quick to drain out of the walls. So I sit beside the waterfall by my glass pyramid, and I visualize all the house bathed in bright sunlight. The brightness grows, shining with such blue-white brilliance that I can no longer see the outline of the building. At last it's a ball of flaming light, too hot for any negativity to endure.

A fountain springs up in the centre of my home, dousing the flames, until the whole house is shining pure and clean in my imagination.

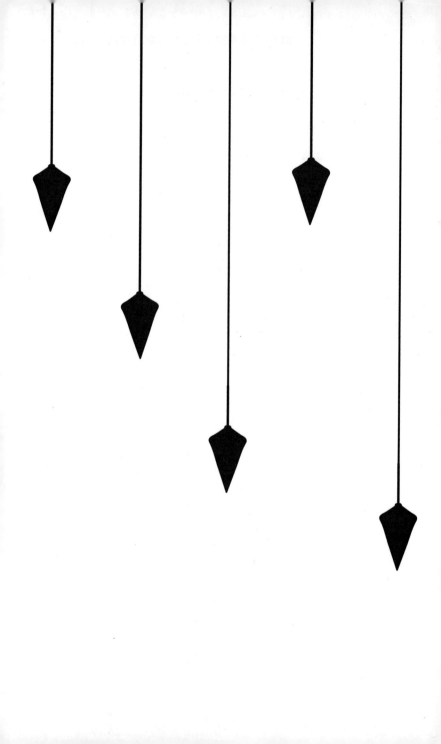

DOWSING FENG SHUI

HOW TO CLEANSE YOUR HOME

If you're house-hunting, take your pendulum along with you. Don't be shy about asking blunt questions: "Will we be happy here?" "Is this the right house for us?" Rely on your subconscious – it's best at making instinctive decisions, because that's its job. Use your intuitive forces.

Many dowsers can detect streams of energy criss-crossing the Earth's surface. If positive energy is rushing through your future home, you'll feel enthusiastic and upbeat as you step over the threshold. But sometimes energy streams can bring negativity, especially if ugly buildings are blocking the flow nearby. Cats are said to love negative energy, by the way: they transform it. So if you think there's negativity in your home, maybe you need a cat (though personally, I'm a dog man!).

If your choices are limited and you have to move into a house despite misgivings about negative energy or bad vibes, you might consider employing a professional dowser to track down your problems. In Britain you can talk to the British Society of Dowsers and they'll put you in touch with someone like Ray and

Ann Procter, in Somerset, who specialize in "healing" houses. The couple are in their eighties – Ray is a retired aeronautical engineer – and they say they've healed more than 10,000 homes in 40 years, helping to relieve their owners of long-term problems such as depression and migraine.

Always use prayer and meditation with your pendulum to cleanse a place when you first move in. Repeat the rituals regularly to protect yourself and the ones you love from negative energies. Meditations work most intensely when more than one sense is invoked. I always touch something powerful, often a crystal, when I focus on visualizations. So why not maximize your prayers by utilizing all your senses and carrying your pendulum?

First, choose some inspirational music. I love Vivaldi and Mozart for prayers – but Pink Floyd works for me too. Place a glass of juice or water in every room, and a few segments or pieces of fruit. As you walk through the house, enhance your meditation with a sip or a bite, and savour the texture and flavours on your tongue.

Keep something near to you that is precious. A pet is ideal, because you'll be pouring out love and receiving unconditional love in return. Crystals and sacred books are also a great choice, and I even have a friend who carries her favourite paperweight, a plastic snowstorm from New York, which she shakes in every room!

Burn your favourite incense sticks or perfumed candles to activate your sense of smell. Peppermint is a perfect odour for cleansing. And use your eyes: look intently at the shape and the lines of your home, especially the way that the light floods through the windows or shines from the lamps.

That's five senses unleashed. Now say a prayer and release the most powerful sense of all. Hold your pendulum and ask it to react positively as you pray: it's great to watch the crystal swing, as though it's broadcasting your prayer throughout the room.

Uri's mini-class

Try my favourite prayer: "Let this place be filled from floor to ceiling with light, harmony and love." Repeat it in every room with a crystal cupped in your palms.

True stories

Dowser Kenneth Merrylees was an "experimental officer" in the Bomb Disposal Squad during World War II. He used his skills to find bombs with delayed-action fuses that had burrowed underground. Colonel Merrylees could find explosives 50ft (15m) below the surface, and saved Buckingham Palace when he detected an unexploded 500-lb (227-kg) bomb under the palace swimming pool. "I find it impossible to accept a purely physical explanation of the dowser's ability," he said. "I am forced to look beyond the limitations of orthodox physics and the five senses."

HOW TO DECORATE BY DOWSING

My daughter Natalie once shared a small apartment in London with a friend who was training to be a singer. It was just a little place, but there was something about that flat that was so joyful and fun-filled – it couldn't be explained simply by the light that streamed in through the south-facing windows. My wife commented on how happy the place felt, and Nat answered sagely, "That's because we're always singing in here."

She was so right, because it isn't just chairs, tables and books that furnish a room. The essential ingredient is spirit. Fill a house with cheerful noises and it will zing with energy. That's why a home where young children are allowed to play happily will always seem perfectly furnished, even if there are milk stains on the sofa and jam all over the telly.

Use your dowsing instincts when you decorate a room. Before reaching for the paintbrush, pick up your pendulum and ask if your energy is able to flow as perfectly as possible right now. If the answer is "Yes", then you're lucky! If not, ask what is blocking the flow: is it the colour, is it the clutter, is it the memories?

To pick the best colour for a room, simply collect some paint charts from a DIY store. Ask your crystal, "Will this room be best in shades of yellow? Green? Pink?" When you've narrowed it down, work your way through the subtle gradations of colour on the charts: "Shocking pink? Suffolk pink? Salmon pink?" Your subconscious will generate some fascinating colour combinations that you might never have considered.

Clearing clutter can be a challenge. Don't be tempted to be too ruthless – if you tidy a room with a bulldozer, you'll sweep away much that you'll wish you had kept. Instead, place your hand on each object and ask your pendulum, "Do I want to keep this?" That can be a difficult question, so allow yourself to relax into a meditative state and let the answer come in its own time. If your crystal shows that you can't bear to throw the thing away, ask if you want to keep it out, on display. You'll soon have three piles: things to throw away, things to keep on display and things to store out of sight.

This technique is especially valuable when you're ridding a room of memories that sap your energy. If you have photos of relatives, perhaps ones who have passed away, on your walls, it would be wrong to throw them out – but your dowsing skill might reveal you'll be happier when you're not always living under the eyes of the past.

Uri's mini-class

Use the four elements (fire, earth, water and air) to sharpen up a room's energies. Burn scented candles, especially sage and lavender. Place an egg and a handful of salt, both of them "earth" elementals, in a dish in the room overnight, to absorb negative energies. Under a tap scatter the salt and break the egg to disperse the energies. Fill an atomizer with water, and pray over it for a few minutes, filling it with healing thoughts and wishes. Then spray the water around the room. Fill the air with song and melody. If, like me, you've got a terrible voice, play some soothing music. I'm lucky – I can ask Natalie to pop by and sing for a while!

Put an egg in a room overnight to absorb negative energies, then break the egg into running water to disperse the energies.

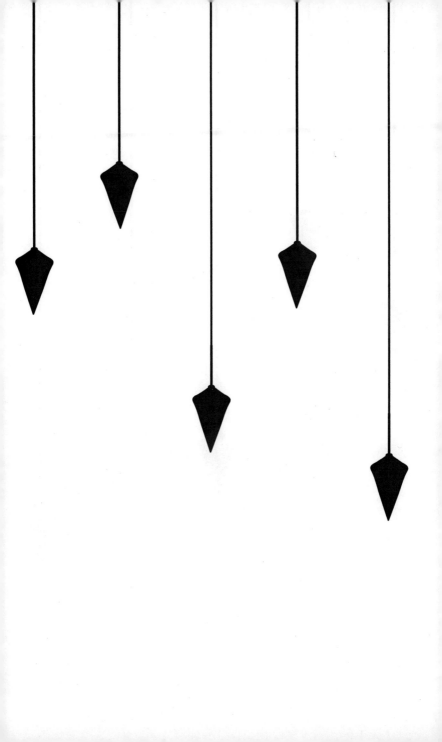

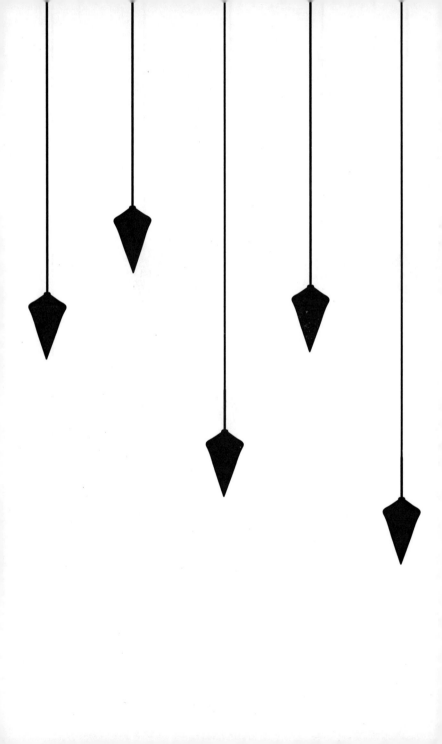

USING A PENDULUM

DOWSING WITH AN ENNEAGRAM

An enneagram is a nine-pointed star that was a sacred symbol long before we learned to write. It makes a fascinating dowsing tool, too.

Around the points of the enneagram place nine questions. You could write them on folded slips, or just signify each question by a word. Here I've put the names of the nine human personality types on the diagram, as an experiment.

Take a stone that attracts you and place it on the first point. Hold your pendulum over the centre of the diagram and ask: "Am I this type of person?" Feel the response of your pendulum and make a note of it. Move the stone to the next point on the diagram and ask the same question. Repeat the process for all the other points on the diagram. Don't be surprised if your pendulum gave more than one "yes" response. We all have elements of more than one personality type: the ancients believed a perfect soul would display all nine.

If the names of the types mean nothing to you, here's a quick guide:

Reformer – opinionated, dogmatic, determined

Mother hen – protective, loving, defensive

Actor – flamboyant, manipulative, extrovert

Artist – deep, wary, introvert

Observer – detached, guarded, deep-thinking

Believer – loyal, gregarious, a team player

Busy bee – energetic, driven, scatty

Boss – a leader, risk-taker, poor at details

Magician – cooperative, creative, a harmonizer

DOWSING WITH TIME CHARTS

Sometimes it's as important to know "when" as "where". A dowsing chart represents the divisions of a 24-hour clock, and it can help you discover the best time to tackle a task, the approximate time that you lost a missing item or the time a wayward spouse or child can be expected to stagger through the door tonight!
Use the chart just as you do the enneagram: take a

stone, crystal or any small object that has significance
for you and place it on an hour of the clock. Hold your
pendulum over the chart and ask, "Is this the time when ...?"

Draw similar charts for the days of a lunar cycle
or even the weeks of the year. Here's a tip for a year
chart: don't try to cram 52 divisions into your circle.
Slice it into twelve months instead and have a second
chart with six full weeks to represent the months ... yes,
six, not four, as February is the only month which ever
divides neatly into four sets of seven days. Most months
begin partway through one week, run through four
more, and sometimes even break into a sixth.

When you draw a seven-sectioned circle to represent
the days of the week, it's up to you whether the week
begins on a Sunday or a Monday or any other day. I'm
Jewish, and our Sabbath is Saturday.

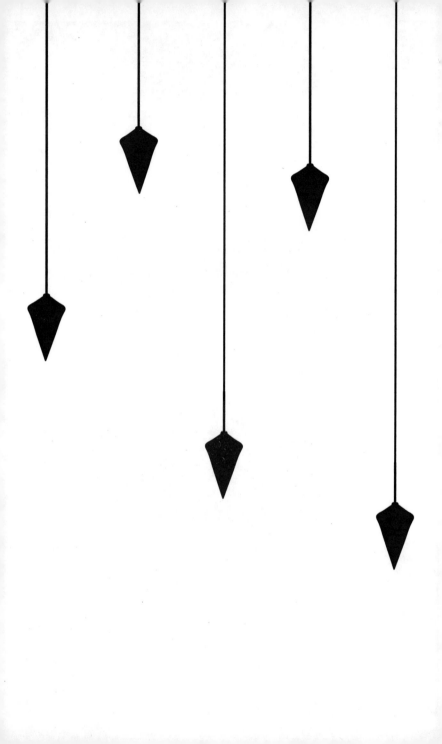

DOWSING WITHOUT
INSTRUMENTS

EVERYTHING IS AT YOUR FINGERTIPS

Try this and amaze yourself. Take a piece of paper. Cut a square about 2in (5cm) on each side and fold it from top to bottom. Open it up again. Fold it from side to side and open it up again. You now have a square piece of paper creased into four smaller squares. Fold it from corner to corner, open it and fold it along the other diagonal, corner to corner. Now you have a square divided into eight triangles. Pinching it along the diagonals, push it into a star shape.

Take a needle and a little ball of Blu Tac® (Poster Putty®). Stick the eye of the needle into the Blu Tac, so the sharp tip points straight up, and place the paper star on it like a hat. The needle's point should be at the centre of the paper where the creases meet, without piercing it, so the star balances. A light breath or a touch of the finger will set the star spinning smoothly.

Here's the amazing part. Without touching it or breathing on it, simply by cupping your hands around it, you can make the star spin. This is not air currents or body heat or sleight of hand or magic. It is psychic power.

Put your paper spinner on a table and sit in front of it. Bring your open palms toward the star. Curl your fingers around the spinner. Stare at it and breathe evenly and lightly. Gently will the star to turn. Urge it silently with your mind. For 30 seconds or so it is likely that nothing will happen. Then the star may start on its axis, very slowly, probably in an anticlockwise direction.

Incredibly, about 60 per cent of people will be able to perform this feat of psychokinesis. Many of you will find that you don't get a result immediately, but success comes after two or three days of attempts. So keep trying! When it happens it's mind-blowing, the clearest demonstration you'll ever see that we all possess psychokinetic energy.

The hands are our bodies' strongest psychic conductors. That's where our life force flows most powerfully. Learn to channel it through the simple spinning pattern of the paper spinner and you could feel enormous physical benefits.

This force is closely linked to dowsing energy. Don't worry if you can't make the paper star spin straight away – it takes concentration, faith and practice, and every human being's energy field is unique, so results always vary wildly. One thing is sure: the more you focus on learning to dowse with a pendulum, the better you'll get at spinning the star.

True stories

In 2015 animal navigation expert Richard Nissen challenged 17 dowsers to map dowse the migratory paths of fledgling cuckoos. Within 15 minutes all but one of the group had plotted cuckoo flyways from Britain to the Congo that accurately matched those mapped by the British Trust for Ornithology.

AND FINALLY ...

Here we are at the end of the book, which means either that you are to be congratulated for patiently absorbing all the lessons and exercises from start to finish, or that like me you always read the last page first to find out whodunnit.

As you learn to dowse, you discover that everything you need is literally in your hands. The science behind it is barely understood – in the 1960s a Dutch geologist called Solco Tromp reported that dowsers were sensitive to minute fluctuations in the Earth's magnetic field, which could be caused by the presence of flowing water or metal deposits. That's just one of many theories, and it doesn't begin to explain what makes the rods twitch or the pendulum spin.

I believe that the science is less important. After all, more than 300 years after an apple bounced off Sir Isaac Newton's head, we still don't know how gravity works. The most powerful telescopes are unable to find the "gravity waves" that Einstein predicted. But we still stick to the planet, just as the sun rose even when high priests claimed it was a blazing chariot pulled by fire horses.

All you need to know is this: be positive, believe in yourself and your dowsing skill will develop. Enjoy yourself as you practise and experiment. When it doesn't work, shrug it off and try again. When you have success, enjoy it. Listen to your intuitions – as your dowsing power increases, your instincts will communicate more forcefully. You'll learn to feel the answers even as you begin to phrase the questions. When you're an experienced pendulum dowser, you'll often find the crystal starts to swing as soon as you pick it up ... our thoughts, after all, move at the speed of light.

If you enjoy working with a forked stick, you'll develop an appreciation of the trees whose wood suits you. If you use angle rods, you'll find some metals work better than others. If you work with a crystal, you'll realize that some stones seem to shine like beacons while others remain inert lumps. And if, like me, you're most sensitive when working with your bare hands, you'll acquire a new awareness of all physical sensations, which is often sensual but which also sometimes feels as if you've been sunburned from head to toe.

Respect your talent. Use it for good, to make your life better and to help the people you love.

Enjoy your talent. Remember that our psychic skills are keenest when we're having fun. A childlike outlook will supercharge your dowsing power.

Be proud of your talent. It's one of the wonderful things about being human. It feels great and it's free. Who could ask for more?

Send your prayers for humanity out to the world. I believe that we are all connected to each other with an invisible spiritual thread along which we can send emotions, prayers, healing and the power of love. Remember: stay positive, be optimistic, believe in yourself and have faith. With this book I wish you health, happiness and peace of mind. I send you tons of positive energy and love.

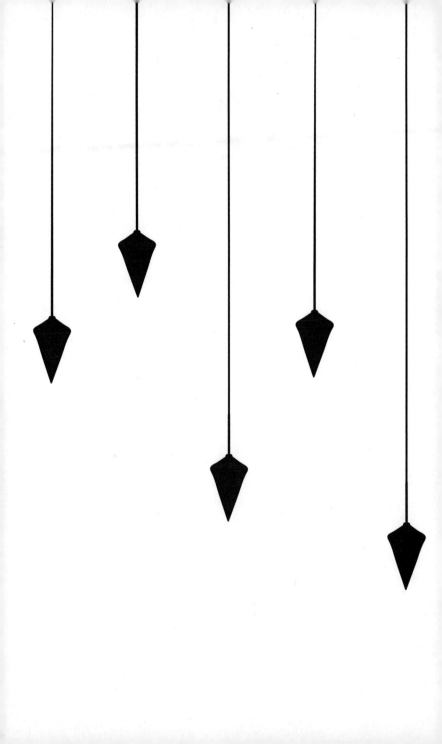

About
Uri Geller

Uri Geller is the world's most investigated and celebrated paranormalist. Famous around the globe for his mind-bending psychic powers, he has led a unique life shrouded in debate, controversy and mystery. In 2017 the CIA released files describing tests of Uri's abilities that led scientists at Stanford Research Institute to conclude "he has demonstrated his paranormal perceptual ability in a convincing and unambiguous manner". The results were published in the prestigious science magazine *Nature*.

As well as using his gifts to detect oil and precious metals, Uri works as a motivational MindPower coach to leading sports men and women and industrialists. He has lectured at the United Nations and to the directors and CEOs of large multinational companies, such as Google, Reuters, Novartis, Mizuno, Sony, Rolls Royce, PwC, Hallmark and many more. He was also invited to speak at the World Economic Forum at Davos, Switzerland.

During the Cold War, at the request of the US Department of Defense, Uri used his telepathic skills to successfully influence the Russians to sign a nuclear arms treaty. He also helped to negotiate an agreement between the Red Cross, the Palestine Red Crescent and the Magen David Adom, Israel's emergency relief service, and was involved in discussions to secure Israel's membership of the Red Cross movement. His tireless dedication to raising funds for charity led him to set up the Uri Geller Charitable Foundation, which supports the many causes that are close to his heart, such as Great Ormond Street Hospital, Make a Wish Israel and The Young Lives Foundation.

The creator and star of multiple hit TV shows and live events seen around the world, Uri is also the subject of a BBC documentary by Oscar-winning director Vikram Jayanti and of a book by master biographer Jonathan Margolis.

A keen artist, Uri's drawings, paintings and artworks have been exhibited in the USA, Europe, Japan and Israel. He also creates pottery, glass and natural rock crystal jewellery. The new Uri Geller Museum in Old Jaffa, Israel, has been built to showcase items from his extensive collection, including an 60ft (18.5m) spoon that weighs 11 tonnes and has been officially certified by Guinness World Records as the largest spoon in the world.

He is the father of a son and a daughter and the author of numerous books on a wide variety of subjects.

Write to him at *uri@urigeller.com* and visit his website: *www.urigeller.com.*

Selected testimonials

"I was shocked and amazed how Mr Geller bent my office key at MIT while I was holding it. The sturdy key kept bending in my hand; I cannot explain this phenomenon – I can only assume that it could relate to quantum chromodynamics."
Dr Victor Weisskopf (Professor of Physics, Massachusetts Institute of Technology, Cambridge, USA)

"I was in scientific laboratories at Stanford Research Institute investigating a rather amazing individual named Uri Geller. Uri's ability to perform amazing feats of mental wizardry is known the world over. We in science are just now catching up and understanding what you can do with exercise and proper practice. Uri is *not* a magician. He is using capabilities that we all have and can develop with exercise and practice."
Dr Edgar D Mitchell SCD (astronaut)

"As a result of Geller's success in this experimental period, we consider that he has demonstrated his paranormal perceptual ability in a convincing and unambiguous manner."
Dr Harold Puthoff and Dr Russell Targ (Stanford Research Institute, USA)

"I think Uri is a magician, but I don't particularly believe that he is using trickery. I believe there are psychic abilities. They don't accord with any science we have at the moment, but maybe some future science will back them up with theories."
Dr Brian Josephson (Professor of Physics, University of Cambridge, and winner of the 1973 Nobel Prize for Physics)

"Geller has bent my ring in the palm of my hand without ever touching it. Personally, I have no scientific explanation for the phenomena."
Dr Wernher von Braun (NASA scientist and pioneer of rocket technology)

"I met Mr Geller while he was being studied at Stanford Research Institute. During our conversation he demonstrated his mind-reading techniques and plucked out of my mind an image I was thinking of; it was very impressive."
George Edward Pake (former president of the American Physical Society and member of the President of the United States' Science Advisory Committee)

"As a result of this personally witnessed experiment in clear unequivocal conditions I am able to state with confidence my view that Mr Geller has genuine psychic capability."
Arthur Ellison (Emeritus Professor of Electrical Engineering, City, University of London)

Books by Uri Geller

My Story (Praeger/Robson), 1975
The Geller Effect (Henry Holt/Jonathan Cape/Grafton),
1986
Uri Geller's Fortune Secrets (Sphere), 1987
Shawn (Goodyer Associates), 1990
Change Your Life in One Day (Marshall Cavendish),
1990
Uri Geller's MindPower Kit (Penguin/Virgin), 1996
Uri Geller's Little Book of Mind Power (Robson), 1998
Ella (Headline Feature), 1998
Dead Cold (Headline Feature), 1999
Mind Medicine (Chrysalis), 1999
Uri Geller's ParaScience Pack (van der Meer), 2000
Unorthodox Encounters (Robson), 2001
Confessions of a Rabbi and a Psychic (Robson/
Source), 2001
Uri Geller's Life Signs (Reader's Digest), 2002

Index

Notes

....

....

....

....

....

....

....

WATKINS

Sharing Wisdom Since 1893

The story of Watkins began in 1893, when scholar of esotericism John Watkins founded our bookshop, inspired by the lament of his friend and teacher Madame Blavatsky that there was nowhere in London to buy books on mysticism, occultism or metaphysics. That moment marked the birth of Watkins, soon to become the publisher of many of the leading lights of spiritual literature, including Carl Jung, Rudolf Steiner, Alice Bailey and Chögyam Trungpa.

Today, the passion at Watkins Publishing for vigorous questioning is still resolute. Our stimulating and groundbreaking list ranges from ancient traditions and complementary medicine to the latest ideas about personal development, holistic wellbeing and consciousness exploration. We remain at the cutting edge, committed to publishing books that change lives.

DISCOVER MORE AT:

www.watkinspublishing.com

Read our blog

Watch and listen to
our authors in action

Sign up to
our mailing list

We celebrate conscious, passionate, wise and happy living.
Be part of that community by visiting

 /watkinspublishing   @watkinswisdom

 /watkinsbooks   @watkinswisdom